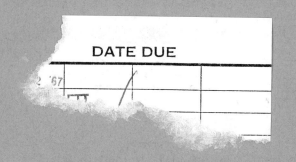

DATE DUE

2 '67

MR

The Art of

AFRICA

Shirley Glubok

Designed by Gerard Nook
Special Photography by Alfred H. Tamarin

HARPER & ROW, PUBLISHERS • NEW YORK

THE AUTHOR GRATEFULLY ACKNOWLEDGES THE ASSISTANCE OF:

ALLAN D. CHAPMAN, Librarian, The Museum of Primitive Art
WARREN M. ROBBINS, Director, Museum of African Art
FREDERICK BROWN, African-American Institute
JIMMY and PAUL SCHNELL

AND ESPECIALLY THE HELPFUL COOPERATION OF:

TAMARA NORTHERN, Research Assistant, The Museum of Primitive Art

Other Books by SHIRLEY GLUBOK:
THE ART OF ANCIENT EGYPT
THE ART OF LANDS IN THE BIBLE
THE ART OF ANCIENT GREECE
THE ART OF THE NORTH AMERICAN INDIAN
THE ART OF THE ESKIMO
THE ART OF ANCIENT ROME

Africa is an enormous continent. The Sahara Desert in the north sets apart the countries near the Mediterranean Sea from the vast lands to the south. South of the Sahara the great African continent stretches from seashores to snow-capped mountains, from jungles and forests to vast grasslands, from mighty rivers and waterfalls to empty deserts and volcanoes.

Millions of people live south of the Sahara. They belong to hundreds of tribes, all with different styles of art. Most African art is made for religious ceremonies. The tribesmen call on spirits and try to control supernatural powers. The ceremonies are closely connected with daily life, with planting, harvesting, having children, and hunting. Some African art was made to praise powerful kings and tribal chiefs.

More than five hundred years ago Yoruba kings, called Oni, were ruling in the capital city of Ife in Nigeria. On the left is a bronze head of an Oni of Ife wearing a beaded crown with a plume. The grooves may represent the tribal scars that Ife kings put on their faces.

Ife artists were masters at *casting,* or forming, bronze sculpture. They knew how to cast bronze long before the first Europeans, the Portuguese, arrived in 1472.

Later kings in Nigeria, called Obas, lived in the city of Benin in magnificent walled palaces. Live leopards were often captured for the king, then tamed and kept in the palace. At the right is a royal leopard made of five elephant tusks. The spots are made of copper.

The Kingdom of Benin in Nigeria lasted more than five centuries. Its art was almost unknown to the outside world until 1897, when a British expedition captured Benin City and took many of the masterpieces back to England. Soon people everywhere came to know the beautiful bronzes and ivories. Ancient Nigerian art now ranks with the great art of the world.

This bronze statue was found in Benin City in 1897, but it may have been made nearby in another part of Nigeria. A hunter is carrying home an antelope, which he shot with his bow and arrow. The bended knees show the weight of the antelope and the weariness of the hunter.

6

This mask, one of the finest ivory carvings in the world, was owned by the king of Benin when the British captured the city. The mask is six inches high. The king wore it as an ornament on his chest. Little carved heads of bearded Portuguese men form the crown. The eyes and the strips on the forehead were once inlaid with copper.

Ivory from the tusks of elephants was highly prized by Benin kings.

Ivory can be carved to show fine detail in *relief*. A relief is a raised picture that stands out from the background. Benin carvers used ivory for both low and high reliefs. The coral net cap on this head is carved in low relief, while the nose and mouth are in high relief.

Pillars and walls of the Benin royal palaces were decorated with hundreds of bronze reliefs showing heroic deeds of the kings and life in the palace. The king, standing proudly in the center of this bronze plaque, is wearing a high collar of coral beads, a sign of royalty. A servant is holding up one of his hands. The servants were made very small to show that they were unimportant. The larger figures on each side are high officers. They are holding up palm leaves to shield the king from the sun.

This plaque, like all Benin bronzes, was cast by the *lost-wax method* of bronze casting. The lost-wax method has been known since very early times and is still being used today.

First the artist makes a rough model out of earth. Over this core he makes a wax model, in exactly the shape he wants his figures to be. The wax can be modeled with great care, down to tiny details. When the figure is hard, it is covered with a coating of clay. The whole mold is then heated in a furnace, and the layer of wax melts away. Melted bronze is poured into the empty space where the wax had been. After the figure cools, the outside clay mold is removed. The bronze statue can then be polished.

9

Masks are very important in all African tribal ceremonies. Most masks are worn by members of secret societies, groups that run the affairs of the tribe. A main purpose of a secret society is to train boys and girls for their duties as adults. Secret society members wear masks for their dancing ceremonies. They call on spirits to keep evil forces away. It is believed that a man can stop being himself and become a spirit for a short time when he disguises himself in a mask and costume. The spirit would enter the man and speak through him.

On the left is a mask from the Basonge tribe in the Congo (Léopoldville). A costume was attached through the holes on the sides and bottom. The mask at the right, also from the Congo, was made by the Baluba tribe. Africans often use the same mask on many different occasions. These masks may have been worn when worshiping ancestors or in time of great danger.

The University Museum, University of Pennsylvan

These two strange looking heads are headdresses made by the Ekoi in the grasslands of Cameroon and Nigeria. The heads were attached to basketwork caps so they could be worn. Members of a secret society of the Ekoi used the headdresses for dances held in connection with great festivals and funerals.

Ekoi heads are startling. The marks painted on the faces represent tattooing, to show the wearer's rank in a secret society. Bone teeth make the faces look real.

The heads were carved of soft wood, with antelope or monkey skin stretched over it. To remove the hair, the skin was treated with sap from a secret tree in the forest, then rolled in a banana leaf and taken to the home of the mask maker, where it was hung on the roof to dry. Then the skin was pressed onto the mask with heated metal.

Both men and women are represented in Ekoi masks. These two are white to show that they represent women. Male masks are painted black. Colors have special meaning in African art. For most tribes white is a sign of death.

Some African masks are huge, weighing as much as eighty pounds, while others, usually worn by women and children, are small. Some hide just the face. Others cover the entire head.

Some masks are crudely made, to be used once and thrown away right after the ceremony. Others are carved with great care. This dance mask was beautifully carved by the Baule tribe in Ivory Coast. It is calm and delicate. The heavy eyelids, long, straight nose, and buttonlike mouth give it charm.

The Baga tribe in Guinea has an important secret society called the Simo. The shoulder mask at the right was used by the society in honor of Nimba, goddess of motherhood. It is almost four feet high. A dancer would put it on over his shoulders. He could see through a small opening between the breasts. His body and legs were hidden by a costume of raffia, long threads of fiber from the leaves of a palm tree. The large head jutting forward from the long, thin neck makes this mask look powerful. This Simo Society mask was an important possession of the tribe.

Headdresses and masks are worn together with costumes of tree fibers and leaves. They are made to be seen in motion. The wearer runs or dances or leaps into the air; sometimes he walks on high stilts. Ceremonies are usually accompanied by chanting and the booming of tribal drums.

16

The Senufo tribe of Ivory Coast has a secret society whose purpose is to drive witches away from the village. The tribesmen wear wooden masks called fire spitters. On the far left is a *detail,* or part, of a fire-spitter mask.

It is said that during the dances, which are held at night, tinder is placed in the mouth of the mask and set on fire. Tinder is a dry material that will catch fire easily and burn quickly. The Senufo tribesman puts a mask on over his head and dresses in a raffia costume. He leaps about, cracking a whip, to the noise of horns. He bellows like a bull and blows sparks out through the jaws.

Nearby in Ghana live the Ashanti. Ashanti women and girls go about with wooden dolls tucked into the backs of their waistcloths, where babies are carried. The dolls are flat with very long necks. They are charms to ensure having good-looking children. A woman carries a round-headed doll if she wants a boy and a square-headed doll if she wants a girl.

This is a fetish from the Basonge tribe. A fetish is a figure that is believed to have power to do magic. A gummy substance is put on the head or stomach to give it this power. A tooth or bits of glass are sometimes added to the substance. Such things as copper strips, nails, snakeskin belts, and leather bands are often attached to the statue to give it extra strength.

The fetish is thought to give protection against illness or evil. It can also protect against danger in journeys or wars or hunting expeditions. Some fetishes are used for evil purposes.

If a fetish does not work, it is broken into pieces or given away to children as a toy. But before it is ever permitted to leave the tribe, its powers have to be taken away.

The Kingdom of Bakuba in the Congo was rich and powerful for almost fifteen hundred years. It is said that they had one hundred and twenty-four kings, whose ancestors were gods. They ruled a federation of eighteen or more tribes. It was the custom to have a seated statue carved in honor of each king during his lifetime. This one was in honor of Kata Mbula, the one hundred and ninth ruler of the Bakuba kingdom. He reigned from 1800 until about 1812.

Kata Mbula is holding the royal drum and wearing a flat crown decorated with cowrie shells, a sign of his godliness. The wooden knife is a symbol of peace. An earlier king outlawed the use of metal knives because it is wrong to kill. A wooden knife became the royal symbol.

Some African tribes have ceremonies to try to see into the future, to seek cures for illness, or to find out whether someone is lying or telling the truth. The tribesmen call on spirits, both good and bad. Works of art are made to hold the power of these spirits.

The Yoruba in Nigeria believe that messages from their gods are received through magic carvings like the kneeling woman holding a covered bowl in the shape of a rooster. Nuts are thrown into the bowl. The nuts fall into a pattern which is believed to be a message from the spirits.

The wooden figure on the right was used in healing ceremonies by a priestess in a women's secret society of the Mende tribe of Sierra Leone. The figure was rubbed with ointment to charge it with magic power. It was believed that she would sway backward or forward to answer questions.

The University Museum, University of Pennsylvania

Thousands of years ago Stone Age men painted pictures in caves or on the rock walls of cliffs. These paintings have been preserved when overhanging rock protected them from the weather.

Above is a copy of a rock painting in Basutoland in southern Africa. A hunter has wounded an animal with his bow and arrow.

On the right is a painting from the Mtoko Cave in Rhodesia. The figures of the men are simple, with large bodies and tiny heads, but the animals are painted carefully. Ancient artists added new pictures over the older ones, so this wall has several layers of paintings.

Musée de l'Homme

Courtesy Frobenius Institute, Frankfurt, German

Prehistoric men believed that pictures were magic and would bring them luck in the hunt. The rock painting above is at Naukluft in South-West Africa. The hunters, with their bows and arrows, are closing in on a small deer. Suddenly a large rhinoceros charges in, frightening the hunters, who run off in all directions.

The colors for rock paintings came from the earth. Minerals and colored

stones were ground into a powder and mixed with animal fat. Black paint was

made from soot or charcoal. Hollow bones made workable brushes.

In the past hundred years Bushmen in southern Africa have made rock and

cave paintings in the same style as these ancient hunting scenes. Bushmen also

painted battles, dances, and various animals, as well as scenes of daily life.

Courtesy Frobenius Institute, Frankfurt, Germany

In the seventeenth century the fierce warriors of the Fon tribe fought many battles against their neighbors. Fon armies conquered Dahomey and the lands around it. They became famous for their corps of women warriors.

Captives were sold to slave traders and shipped to faraway lands. The Fon Kingdom became wealthy and powerful from the slave trade, and the area around Dahomey became known as the Slave Coast.

The Fon tribesmen honored a god of war called Gu. This is an iron statue of the war god Gu holding a long sword. The iron probably came from a ship that was wrecked off the Slave Coast.

The figure is life-size. It is the largest iron statue ever found in Africa. It was in the palace of the last Fon king when the French took over the kingdom in 1897.

The Baule in Ivory Coast make tiny figures out of brass. These brass figures are called gold weights, because they were used on a balance scale for measuring gold dust. Gold dust was used for money.

The brass figures are made by the lost-wax method. They are different weights. If a figure came out of the mold weighing too much, then part of it, perhaps a leg or an arm, was just broken off. If it was made too light, melted metal was added.

This brass figure is a tiny gold weight, less than three and a half inches high. It shows a man dressed for a tribal dance. He is wearing a costume of heavy raffia and a bull mask that fits over his head.

Ghana is just east of Ivory Coast. It was named the Gold Coast by the Portuguese because the Ashanti who met the European explorers were dressed in fine ornaments of gold. Some of the richest gold mines in the world are in Ghana. Over three hundred years ago the Ashanti conquered the people around them and ruled with mighty kings and queens. At one time only the king and queen mother were allowed to

use gold weights. Later other Ashanti people used them to carry on trade. But the royal weights were kept heavier so that the king always received more gold than other people.

The Ashanti cast their gold weights in many different shapes, such as animals, birds, insects, and fish. Some are shaped like men. Others show scenes from everyday life. Sometimes objects such as beetles have a real beetle inside.

African women, like most women all over the world, are interested in beauty. Women in the Congo sleep on neck rests to keep their hair in place. The neck rests are made of wood from the dense forests of the Congo. They are carved in many different shapes. The one below, made by the Baluba, represents the mother of the tribe watching over the sleeping princess. It was a sign of wealth to own a neck rest.

In Cameroon it was a sign of wealth and high rank to own a stool like the one at the right. The homes and belongings of Cameroon chiefs were decorated with great care. A carved stool was an important possession of chiefs and kings, who sat on their stools during the council gatherings. It was believed that harm would befall anyone else who dared to sit on the stool of a nobleman. The Bamum chief's stool at the right is decorated with carvings of captives' heads.

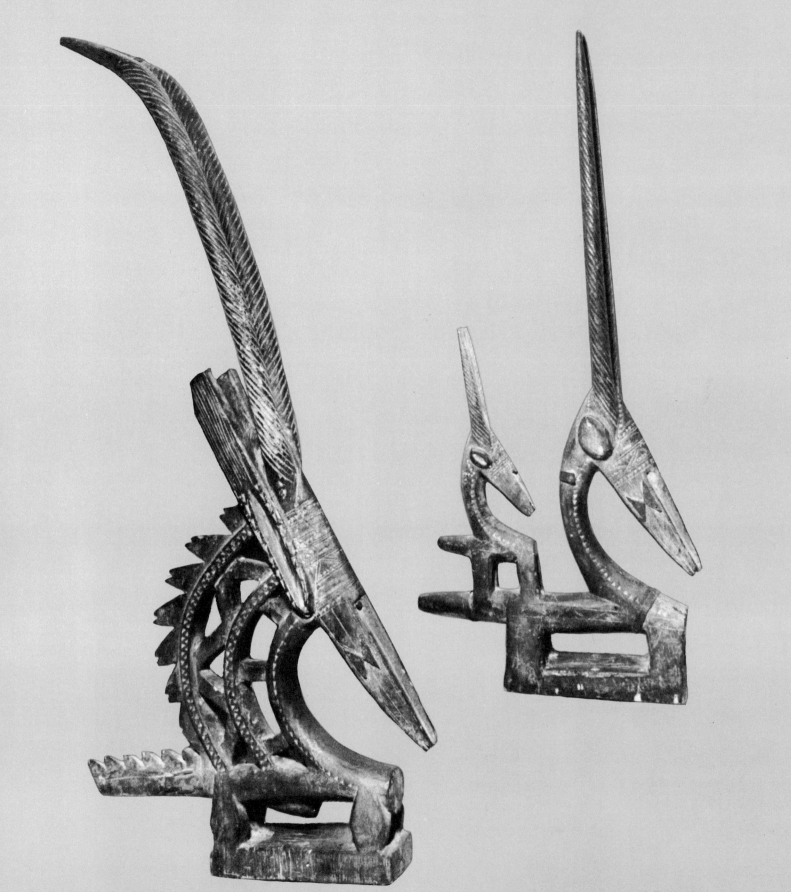

The Bambara tribe lives in the country of Mali. A Bambara story tells that long ago the gods sent them a creature named Chi Wara, to teach them to grow grain. The Bambara make magnificent headdresses shaped like antelopes, which represent Chi Wara. The headdresses are made of light wood and are attached to caps. They are worn at sowing time and at the harvest, in ceremonies to pray for rain and good crops. On the left is a lovely group of Chi Wara antelope headdresses, representing a buck, doe, and fawn.

The Baule tribe holds religious ceremonies to worship their ancestors. The Baule believe that the soul of a loved one leaves the body after death and wanders about the village, looking for a home. A beautiful statue is made to look like the ancestor, who is invited to come live in it. A priest rings bells and shakes rattles, calling to the ancestor, asking him to make a home inside his image. The ancestor figure helps and comforts the family, who talk to it as if it were alive.

Baule carvings are sometimes made as portraits, or likenesses, of living people. A person may sit while his statue is being carved. Or perhaps the artist will cut and carve from memory. The statues may be given to friends and relatives to enjoy.

Special care is taken with the heads, while the bodies are smooth and simple. Tribal scars on the faces and bodies are careful copies from life, as are the fine hairdos. When the carving is finished, the wood is smoothed and polished until it shines. These figures of a seated man and woman, and a woman with her child on her back, are calm and beautiful Baule carvings.

The Baule, like other African tribes, have a style of carving of their own. Young men are trained under master artists for years to learn to make figures like those that were made by tribal artists before them.

Wood is the most popular material used by the Africans. Sculptors carve the trunk or branch fresh from the tree. To the African tribesman wood is a living thing, and cutting and chopping cause it pain. So they beg the spirit of the tree for forgiveness.

Almost all carvings are made from a single piece of wood. The most important tool is the adz, a kind of chisel. A small knife is used to finish the surface.

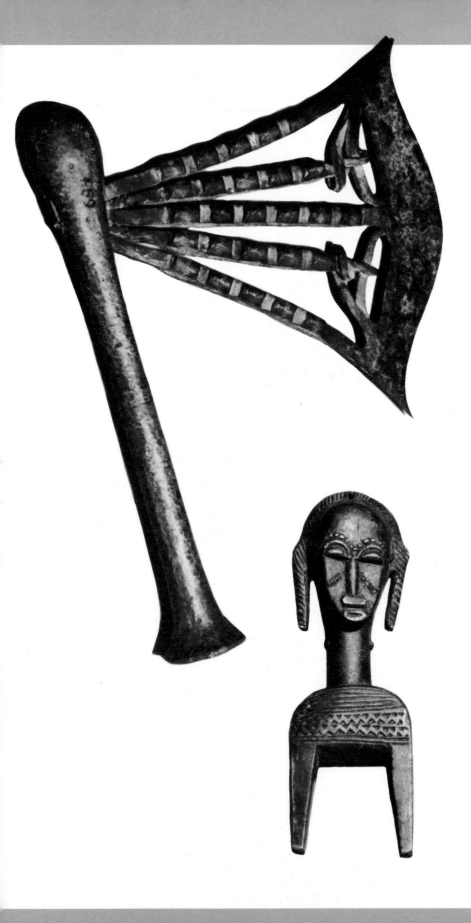

African smiths, or metal workers, have known how to forge iron since ancient times. Iron is forged by heating it in fire and hammering it into shape, then reheating and hammering again and again. This ceremonial ax is made of forged iron. It is from the Basonge tribe in the Congo. The handle of the ax is made of wood and covered with a thin sheet of copper.

Baule artists like to decorate pulley-holders used on looms for weaving. A bar fits across the lower part of the pulley-holder and keeps the thread separated. The face decorating the pulley-holder is thought to be a spirit keeping guard over the work.

American Museum of Natural Hist
Photographs by Alfred H. Tama

The ornamental comb on the left has six very long teeth. It fits into the hair like a hairpin, to keep the hair in place. The comb was made by a member of the Fang tribe in Gabon, a country on the west coast of Africa. It is decorated with the beautiful half figure of a woman, whose long neck is encircled with many rings.

On the right is a metal knife from the Congo (Léopoldville). It was made by the Mangbetu tribe. The wooden handle is in the shape of a head. Long, thin heads and high hairdos are considered beautiful by the Mangbetu, and the heads of little Mangbetu girls were shaped by binding them with strips of cloth.

African pottery makers use simple methods that have been handed down since early times. They shape their pottery by hand. The pots are left in the shade to dry and then baked in an open oven.

The pottery animal above is a hyena, made by the Shilluk tribe in eastern Sudan. The body was covered with a pressed-in decoration and details were left in the dark-brown polished clay.

Most African pottery is made by women, but in the Mangbetu tribe pots in the form of people are made by men. This graceful "kissing pot" was used to pour palm wine or water.

The faces on this pot show scarification, which is thought to be beautiful. Marks are made by punctures or cuts in the skin which form a pattern. Charcoal powder is rubbed into the cuts so they will become scars when they heal. Sometimes scars are made for medical reasons. Medicine is rubbed into the cuts in the hope that it will cure illness.

A gourd is a large fruit with a very hard skin that can be used as a cup or a bottle. The gourd is picked when ripe and soaked in a stream. When the insides rot, the gourd is opened and cleaned out. After the rind has been dried in the sun, it can be decorated. A vessel made of the rind of a gourd is called a calabash.

The figure of the horseman on this Dahomey gourd drinking cup was made by cutting away the background with a hot knife.

The gourd bottles on the right, made in Kenya by the Kamba tribe, were decorated by engraving, or cutting, the lines into the rind and filling them in with a black material.

The Barotse in Zambia make baskets for household use. The fiber is coiled around and around to build up the shape. Black fiber is woven in with the natural fiber to make an animal pattern.

Cowrie shells have always been valuable to chiefs and kings in Cameroon. The shells are used for ornaments and decorations. At one time they were strung together and used for money. The money was worth more inland, where the shells are scarce, than near the seashore, where the shells are plentiful.

When Europeans settled in Cameroon, they brought glass beads to sell to the tribesmen, who liked them for their bright colors. Kings and chiefs used them to decorate their robes and crowns. One king liked them so much that he had his royal throne covered with colored beads.

This little cloth doll of the Bamum tribe is decorated with beads, and her head and ankles are covered with cowrie shells.

The Yoruba of Nigeria often decorate doors and walls with beautiful carved wooden reliefs. Wild animals, human figures, and mythical beings are popular subjects. In the door panel above, the Yoruba artist has carved two men attacking a huge coiled snake which is devouring a turtle. Several African folktales tell about animals that are devoured by snakes. The artist has framed the scene with a geometric design. He has given different and beautiful surface patterns to the carvings of the turtle, the snake, the swords, and even the men's clothing.

Unlike most African art, Dahomey brass figures have no religious or ceremonial purpose. Until about 1900 they could only be made by special artists for the royal court. Now they are made by many different artists and are sent all over the world.

Dahomey brass figures bounce with life and excitement. Household scenes, royal parades, and animals are favorite subjects. In the group below, a king is sitting in his boat, smoking his long pipe. One of his attendants is holding up an umbrella to protect him from the sun, and others are catching fish for him.

At the right is a young antelope eating a leaf. The surface of the sleek, graceful animal is beautifully decorated. Like other Dahomey brass figures, it was made by the lost-wax method.

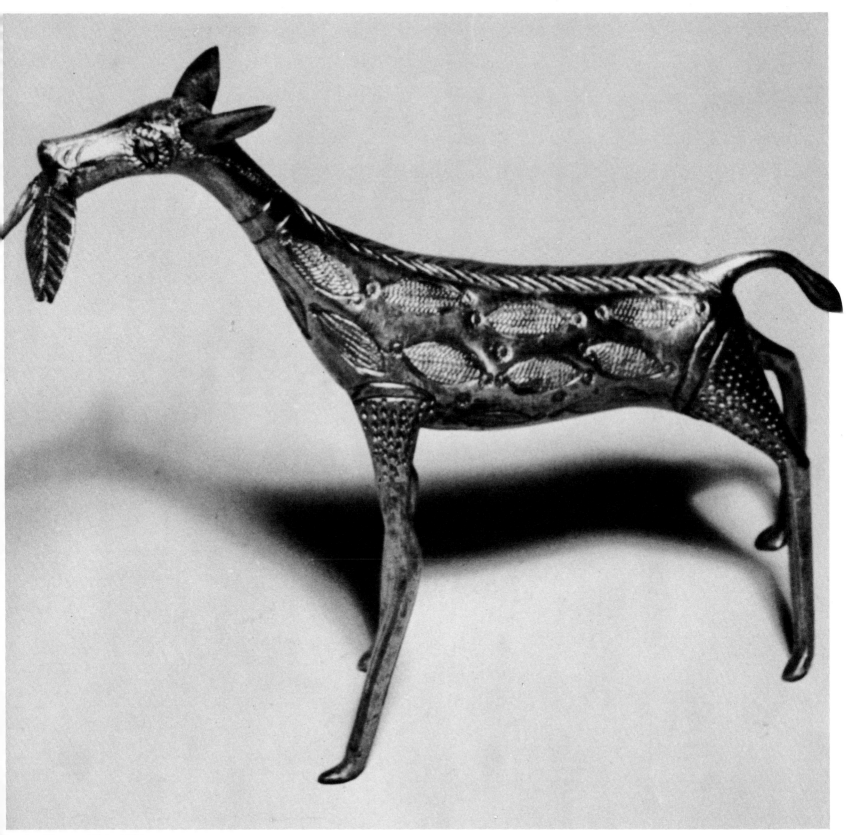

Music is an important part of all African ceremonies. During religious dances tribesmen shake rattles and beat drums. Horns and harps have been played in royal courts since olden times.

The bronze statue at the left represents a horn blower at the court of Benin. It was found by the Europeans in the palace of the last king. This horn is blown from the side.

At the courts of Mangbetu sultans, troubadours

sang and plucked string instruments. They moved about reciting poetry and playing bow harps with five strings. Some of the strings were made of giraffe hair.

The oval-shaped head on this harp—with its tribal scars—is carved in the usual style of Mangbetu art.

The drum was made by the Loango tribe in the Congo (Brazzaville). It has been carved and painted like a statue. A man who is seated on a leopard and holding a child is carrying the drum on his head.

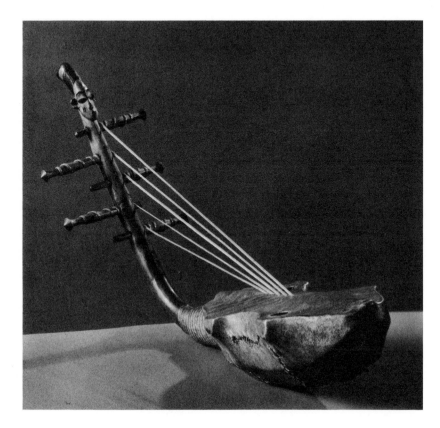

American Museum of Natural History
Photograph courtesy The University Museum

Metropolitan Museum of Art
The Crosby Brown collection of musical instruments, 1889

The forms and styles of African art are centuries old. The arts had been

carried on by the different tribes for a long time.

Yet, until less than a hundred years ago, African art was almost

unknown to people outside Africa.

Its simple beauty expresses the power of nature. When people took

notice of it, African art astonished art lovers everywhere.

Now it has taken its place along with other great art of the world.